EMBRACE
Journal
&
Notebook

McDougal & Associates
Servants of Christ and Stewards of the
Mysteries of God

EMBRACE
Journal
&
Notebook

by

Crystal Callais

Published by:

MCDOUGAL & ASSOCIATES
18896 GREENWELL SPRINGS RD
GREENWELL SPRINGS, LA   70739
WWW.THEPUBLISHEDWORD.COM

McDougal & Associates is dedicated to spreading the Gospel
of the Lord Jesus Christ to as many people as possible
in the shortest time possible.

ISBN 978-1-950398-85-0

Printed on demand in the U.S., the U.K., Australia, and the UAE
For Worldwide Distribution

DEDICATION

I dedicate this book to you, those seeking Jesus and longing to get pulled deeper, feeling the embrace of the Father. I pray that as you spend time journaling, you will feel His sweet embrace saturating your soul.

ACKNOWLEDGMENTS

I want to thank my youth group, Impact, for challenging me in my personal time with Jesus in ways you wouldn't think of.

I thank my family—my husband, my daughters, my parents, and my pastors—for always believing in me and the encouragement you have given over the years.

CONTENTS

The Embrace Journaling Method

E = ENGAGE in a scripture verse or passage that you read or heard.

M = MAIN theme of the passage. Ask yourself what key words stand out or what the motive of the verse was in that culture or within the surrounding verses.

B = BREAK it down. This section is for the meaning of the verse or key words the Lord has highlighted to you. You can also use *Strong's Concordance* to help in a word study or dig into the culture.

R = REVELATION. Write down a summary of what those verses speak to you that you haven't meditated on before.

A = APPLICATION. Write down a practical way you can apply your revelation to a situation, to your life, or to your mind, etc.

C = CHALLENGE yourself. Allow the Holy Spirit to pull you out of your comfort zone, challenging you in a new way, helping you to apply what you have just read.

E = EMBRACE the Father in prayer. Write out or speak to the Father in prayer something related to what you have just read. Pray over the situations and the people of your life that verse applies to, asking the Lord to give you ways to help this scripture not just be something your read, but let it transform your mind and way of living day by day.

INTRODUCTION

Journaling is an important part of a Christian's walk. I was taught to journal as a teenager using a method that consisted of four steps. First, I would find a scripture and write an observation of what that scripture meant to me. Next, I would follow this with an application and observation of that scripture. I would end the thought process with a prayer for the Father to help me apply in my own life what I had read or heard.

As I was meditating and praying for an upcoming youth message, I asked God, "How I can help the youth learn to journal and make it fun? How can I get them (and myself) to search deeper than the surface and learn to love digging deep into the Word?" Because of that prayer, the Lord spoke to my heart several questions to use, and that is where the EMBRACE journaling method was birthed.

I taught the youth that night with six leading questions they had to answer according to the verse they picked. After the service was over, several kids who didn't normally participate came to me and commented that it was the first time they had understood how to journal correctly. Thank You, Lord, for answering prayer.

This journal method was birthed from that prayer and that meeting with the youth. I took the questions the Lord had given me and wrote them in a way that uses the acronym EMBRACE.

I have filled out two sample journal pages in the format in which this study is to be applied. I pray that as you read the Word and apply these principles to your quiet time with the Lord, you would feel the embrace of the Father. Each page is created in such a way that you can color or doodle on it if you choose or just fill out the various sections.

There is also a section at the back of the book for sermon notes. I encourage you to take notes from sermons you hear and then take the verses with your notes and study deeper into them. Do this using the journal pages and the EMBRACE journaling method.

Happy journaling!

Crystal Callais
Houma, Louisiana

I'm absolutely convinced that nothing—nothing living or dead, angelic or demonic, today or tomorrow, high or low, thinkable or unthinkable—absolutely nothing can get between us and God's love because of the way that Jesus our Master has <u>embraced</u> us.
—Romans 8:38-39, MSG

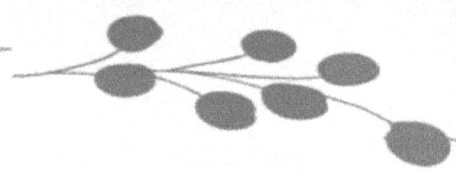

When I am afraid, I put my trust in you. – Psalm 56:3 (NIV)

MAIN THEME OF PASSAGE

Referring to when I am feeling fear. Fear doesn't have to dictate if I trust God or not. Trust isn't an emotion, but something I "put".

BREAK IT DOWN

At the time of this verse, David has been seized by the philistines. Even in the midst of his feelings, he chose to put his trust in God. Trust wasn't something he was feeling.

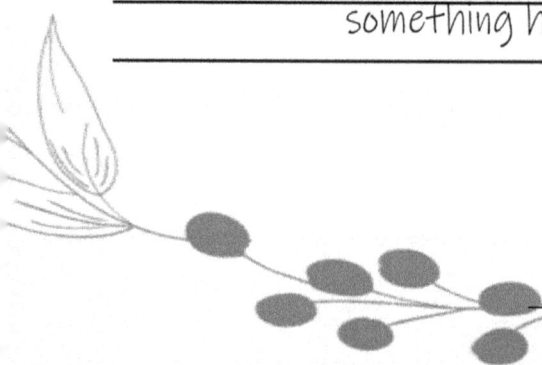

REVELATION

The feelings I felt this week of someone micromanaging me don't have to get under my skin. My Feelings are circumstantial and don't have to dictate my choices! God is big enough to handle my emotions and the circumstance I face.

APPLICATION

- I can pray to see past the emotions when they rise up.
- I can trust that God has my back even when I can't see it.

CHALLENGE

The next time my emotions rise, I will verbally say "I trust God and not my feelings"

EMBRACE IN PRAYER

ENGAGE IN SCRIPTURE

1 Corinthians 13:4-8. (MSG)

Ephesians 5:1-7. (MSG)

MAIN THEME OF PASSAGE

Living a life of love. Paul is encouraging me to walk in love after Christ's example.

BREAK IT DOWN

Love is not a feeling but a choice!
This type of love is a giving of myself.

REVELATION

I am told to LEARN a life of love. I
Can't learn something I already know.

APPLICATION

Rewrite the scripture with my name in it and see if it
describes me. What fruit of love do I not show? I
struggle with not giving up. I can lose hope at times
and grow weary.

CHALLENGE

What is one thing I can do today to
show love in a new way and not give
up so easily?

EMBRACE IN PRAYER

And the LORD answered me and said, Write the vision and engrave it so plainly upon tablets that everyone who passes may [be able to] read [it easily and quickly] as he hastens by.
—Habakkuk 2:2, AMPC

week

1

DAY 1

ENGAGE IN SCRIPTURE

_____
_____
_____
_____

MAIN THEME OF PASSAGE

_____
_____
_____
_____

BREAK IT DOWN

_____
_____
_____
_____

REVELATION

_____
_____
_____
_____
_____

APPLICATION

_____
_____
_____

CHALLENGE

_____
_____
_____
_____
_____

EMBRACE IN PRAYER

DAY 2

ENGAGE IN SCRIPTURE

_____
_____
_____
_____

MAIN THEME OF PASSAGE

_____
_____
_____
_____

BREAK IT DOWN

_____
_____
_____
_____

REVELATION

_____
_____
_____
_____
_____

APPLICATION

_____
_____
_____

CHALLENGE

_____
_____
_____
_____
_____

EMBRACE IN PRAYER

DAY 3

ENGAGE IN
SCRIPTURE

_____

_____

_____

_____

MAIN THEME OF PASSAGE

_____

_____

_____

_____

BREAK IT DOWN

_____

_____

_____

_____

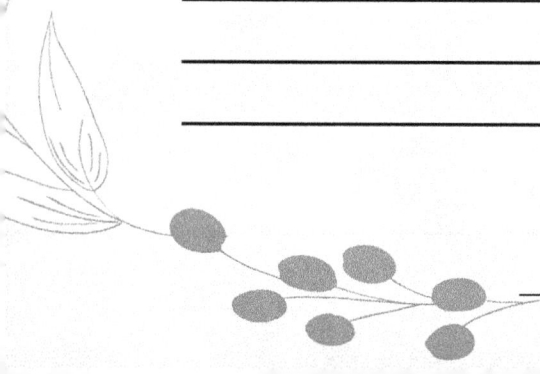

REVELATION

_____
_____
_____
_____
_____

APPLICATION

_____
_____
_____

CHALLENGE

_____
_____
_____
_____
_____

EMBRACE IN PRAYER

DAY 4

ENGAGE IN SCRIPTURE

_____

_____

_____

_____

MAIN THEME OF PASSAGE

_____

_____

_____

_____

BREAK IT DOWN

_____

_____

_____

_____

REVELATION

_____

_____

_____

_____

_____

APPLICATION

_____

_____

_____

CHALLENGE

_____

_____

_____

_____

_____

EMBRACE IN PRAYER

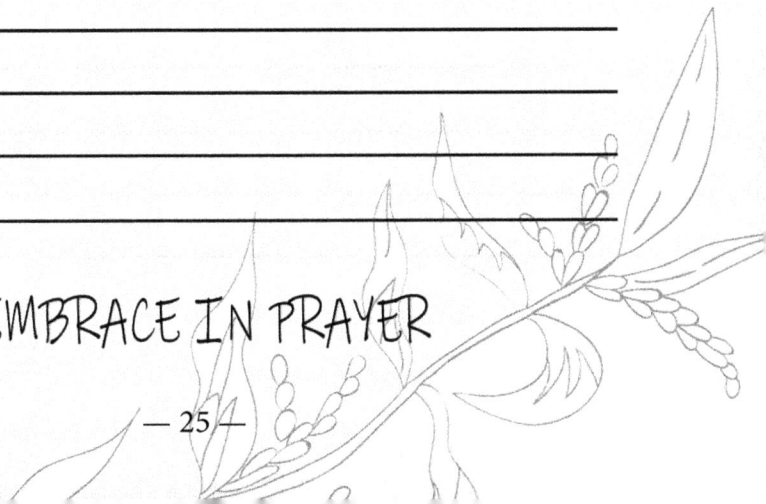

DAY 5

ENGAGE IN SCRIPTURE

_____
_____
_____
_____

MAIN THEME OF PASSAGE

_____
_____
_____
_____

BREAK IT DOWN

_____
_____
_____
_____

REVELATION

_____

_____

_____

_____

APPLICATION

_____

_____

_____

CHALLENGE

_____

_____

_____

_____

EMBRACE IN PRAYER

DAY 6

ENGAGE IN SCRIPTURE

_____
_____
_____
_____

MAIN THEME OF PASSAGE

_____
_____
_____
_____

BREAK IT DOWN

_____
_____
_____
_____

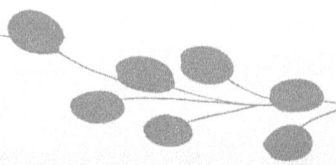

REVELATION

_____
_____
_____
_____
_____

APPLICATION

_____
_____
_____

CHALLENGE

_____
_____
_____
_____
_____

EMBRACE IN PRAYER

ENGAGE IN SCRIPTURE

_____

_____

_____

_____

MAIN THEME OF PASSAGE

_____

_____

_____

_____

BREAK IT DOWN

_____

_____

_____

_____

REVELATION

_____
_____
_____
_____
_____

APPLICATION

_____
_____
_____

CHALLENGE

_____
_____
_____
_____
_____

EMBRACE IN PRAYER

Good friend, don't forget
all I've taught you;
take to heart my commands.
They'll help you live a long,
long time,
a long life lived full and
well.
— Proverbs 3:1-2, MSG

Week

2

DAY 1

ENGAGE IN SCRIPTURE

_____
_____
_____
_____

MAIN THEME OF PASSAGE

_____
_____
_____
_____

BREAK IT DOWN

_____
_____
_____
_____

REVELATION

_____
_____
_____
_____
_____

APPLICATION

_____
_____
_____

CHALLENGE

_____
_____
_____
_____
_____

EMBRACE IN PRAYER

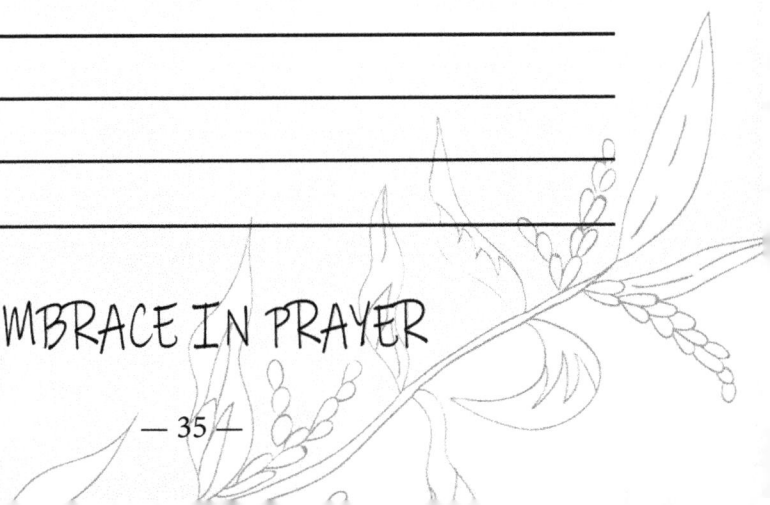

DAY 2

ENGAGE IN
SCRIPTURE

_____
_____
_____
_____

MAIN THEME OF
PASSAGE

_____
_____
_____
_____

BREAK IT DOWN

_____
_____
_____
_____

REVELATION

_____

_____

_____

_____

_____

APPLICATION

_____

_____

_____

CHALLENGE

_____

_____

_____

_____

_____

EMBRACE IN PRAYER

DAY 3

ENGAGE IN SCRIPTURE

_____
_____
_____
_____

MAIN THEME OF PASSAGE

_____
_____
_____
_____

BREAK IT DOWN

_____
_____
_____
_____

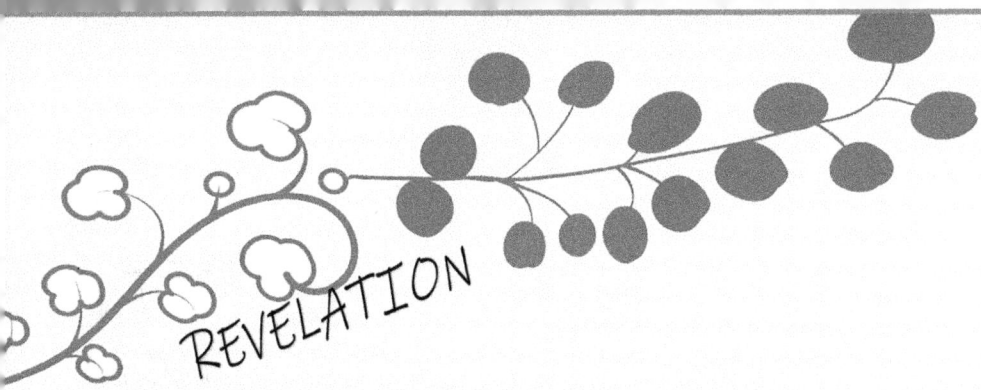

REVELATION

_____
_____
_____
_____
_____

APPLICATION

_____
_____
_____

CHALLENGE

_____
_____
_____
_____
_____

EMBRACE IN PRAYER

DAY 4

ENGAGE IN SCRIPTURE

_____
_____
_____
_____

MAIN THEME OF PASSAGE

_____
_____
_____
_____

BREAK IT DOWN

_____
_____
_____
_____

REVELATION

_____
_____
_____
_____
_____

APPLICATION

_____
_____
_____

CHALLENGE

_____
_____
_____
_____
_____

EMBRACE IN PRAYER

DAY 5

_____
_____
_____
_____

MAIN THEME OF PASSAGE

_____
_____
_____
_____

BREAK IT DOWN

_____
_____
_____
_____

REVELATION

_____
_____
_____
_____
_____

APPLICATION

_____
_____
_____

CHALLENGE

_____
_____
_____
_____
_____

EMBRACE IN PRAYER

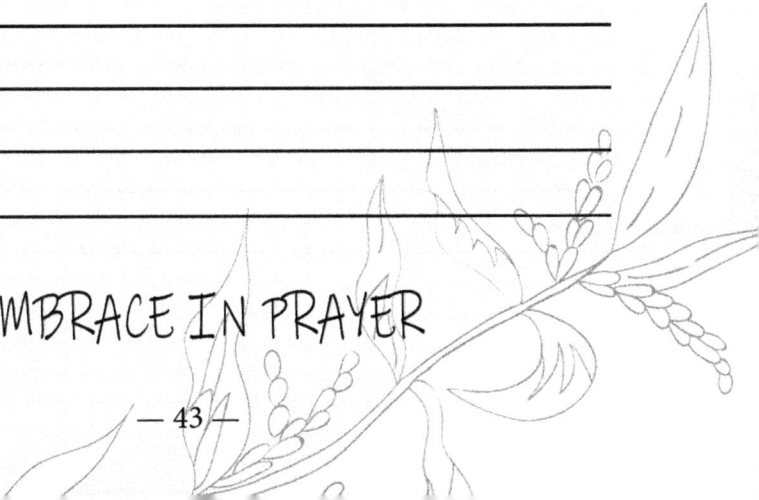

DAY 6

ENGAGE IN SCRIPTURE

_____
_____
_____
_____

MAIN THEME OF PASSAGE

_____
_____
_____
_____

BREAK IT DOWN

_____
_____
_____
_____

REVELATION

_____
_____
_____
_____
_____

APPLICATION

_____
_____
_____

CHALLENGE

_____
_____
_____
_____
_____

EMBRACE IN PRAYER

ENGAGE IN SCRIPTURE

_____
_____
_____
_____

MAIN THEME OF PASSAGE

_____
_____
_____
_____

BREAK IT DOWN

_____
_____
_____
_____

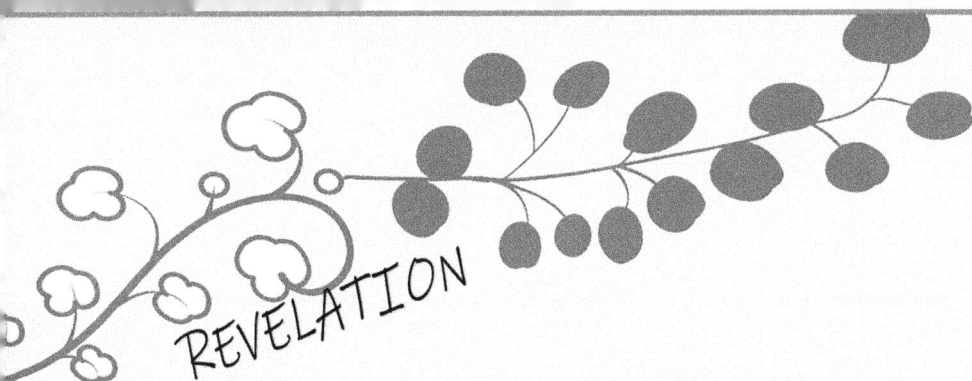

REVELATION

_____
_____
_____
_____
_____

APPLICATION

_____
_____
_____

CHALLENGE

_____
_____
_____
_____
_____

EMBRACE IN PRAYER

This Book of the Law shall not depart out of your mouth, but you shall meditate on it day and night, that you may observe and do according to all that is written in it. For then you shall make your way prosperous, and then you shall deal wisely and have good success.
— Joshua 1:8, AMPC

Week

3

DAY 1

ENGAGE IN SCRIPTURE

_____
_____
_____
_____

MAIN THEME OF PASSAGE

_____
_____
_____
_____

BREAK IT DOWN

_____
_____
_____
_____

REVELATION

_____
_____
_____
_____
_____

APPLICATION

_____
_____
_____

CHALLENGE

_____
_____
_____
_____
_____

EMBRACE IN PRAYER

DAY 2

ENGAGE IN
SCRIPTURE

_____
_____
_____
_____

MAIN THEME OF PASSAGE

_____
_____
_____
_____

BREAK IT DOWN

_____
_____
_____
_____

REVELATION

_____
_____
_____
_____
_____

APPLICATION

_____
_____
_____

CHALLENGE

_____
_____
_____
_____
_____

EMBRACE IN PRAYER

DAY 3

_____
_____
_____
_____

MAIN THEME OF PASSAGE

_____
_____
_____
_____

BREAK IT DOWN

_____
_____
_____
_____

REVELATION

_____

_____

_____

_____

_____

APPLICATION

_____

_____

_____

CHALLENGE

_____

_____

_____

_____

_____

EMBRACE IN PRAYER

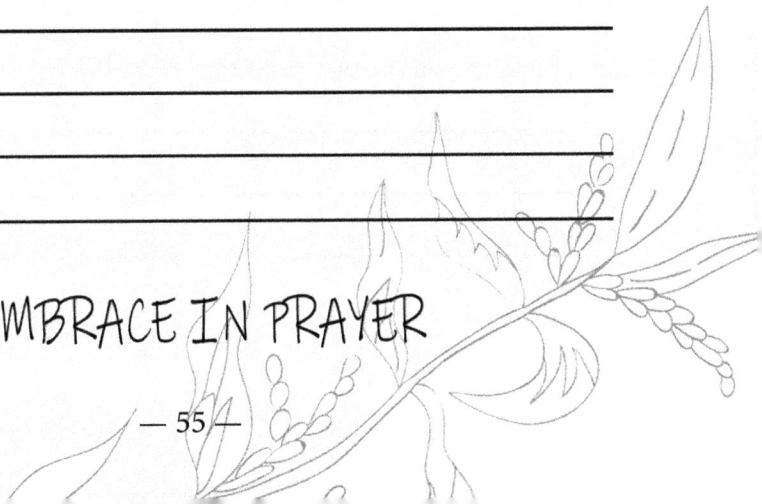

ENGAGE IN SCRIPTURE

_____
_____
_____
_____

MAIN THEME OF PASSAGE

_____
_____
_____
_____

BREAK IT DOWN

_____
_____
_____
_____

REVELATION

_____
_____
_____
_____
_____

APPLICATION

_____
_____
_____

CHALLENGE

_____
_____
_____
_____
_____

EMBRACE IN PRAYER

DAY 5

ENGAGE IN
SCRIPTURE

_____
_____
_____
_____

MAIN THEME OF
PASSAGE

_____
_____
_____
_____

BREAK IT DOWN

_____
_____
_____
_____

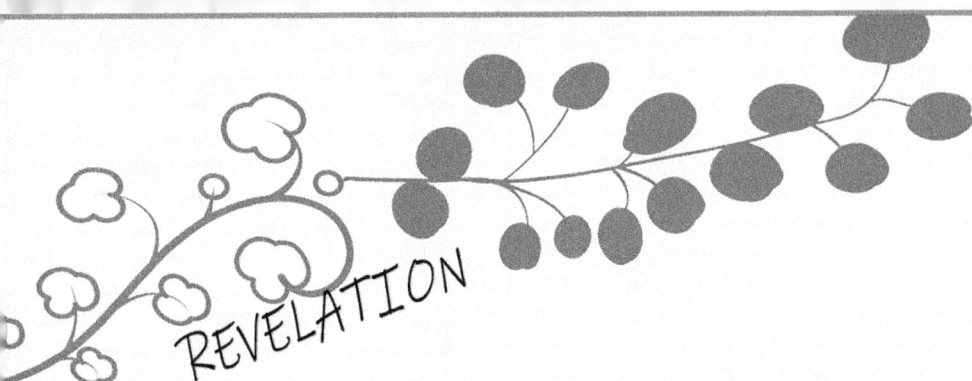

REVELATION

_____
_____
_____
_____
_____

APPLICATION

_____
_____
_____

CHALLENGE

_____
_____
_____
_____

EMBRACE IN PRAYER

DAY 6

ENGAGE IN
SCRIPTURE

_____

_____

_____

_____

MAIN THEME OF
PASSAGE

_____

_____

_____

_____

BREAK IT DOWN

_____

_____

_____

_____

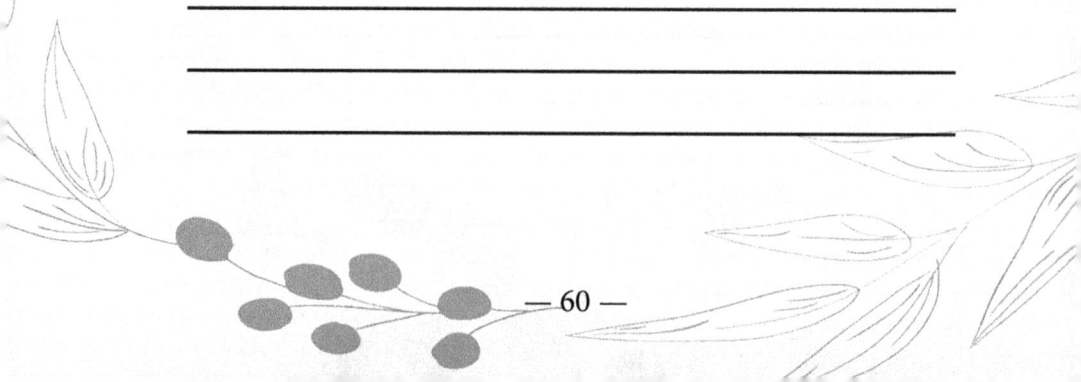

REVELATION

_____
_____
_____
_____
_____

APPLICATION

_____
_____
_____

CHALLENGE

_____
_____
_____
_____
_____

EMBRACE IN PRAYER

ENGAGE IN
SCRIPTURE

_____
_____
_____
_____

MAIN THEME OF
PASSAGE

_____
_____
_____
_____

BREAK IT DOWN

_____
_____
_____
_____

REVELATION

_____
_____
_____
_____
_____

APPLICATION

_____
_____
_____

CHALLENGE

_____
_____
_____
_____
_____

EMBRACE IN PRAYER

Don't be pulled in different directions or worried about a thing. Be saturated in prayer throughout each day, offering your faith-filled requests before God with overflowing gratitude. Tell him every detail of your life, then God's wonderful peace that transcends human understanding, will make the answers known to you through Jesus Christ.
— Philippians 4:6-7, TPT

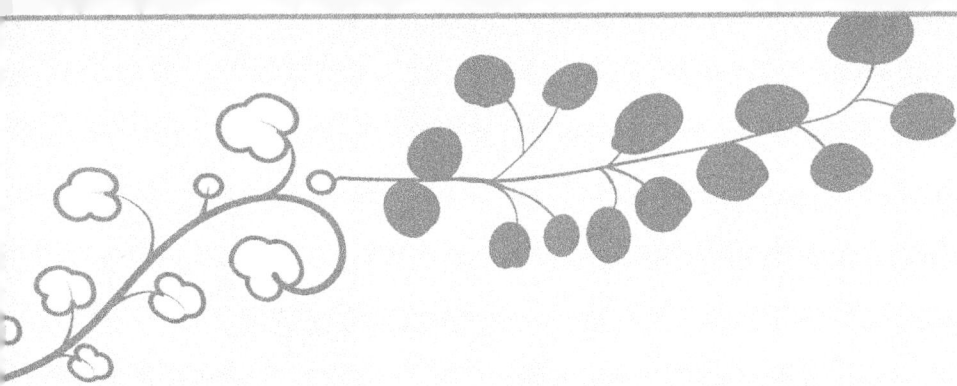

week

4

DAY 1

ENGAGE IN SCRIPTURE

_____
_____
_____
_____

MAIN THEME OF PASSAGE

_____
_____
_____
_____
_____

BREAK IT DOWN

_____
_____
_____
_____

REVELATION

_____
_____
_____
_____
_____

APPLICATION

_____
_____
_____

CHALLENGE

_____
_____
_____
_____
_____

EMBRACE IN PRAYER

DAY 2

ENGAGE IN
SCRIPTURE

_____
_____
_____
_____

MAIN THEME OF PASSAGE

_____
_____
_____
_____

BREAK IT DOWN

_____
_____
_____
_____

REVELATION

_____
_____
_____
_____
_____

APPLICATION

_____
_____
_____

CHALLENGE

_____
_____
_____
_____
_____

EMBRACE IN PRAYER

DAY 3

_____
_____
_____
_____

MAIN THEME OF PASSAGE

_____
_____
_____
_____

BREAK IT DOWN

_____
_____
_____
_____

REVELATION

_____
_____
_____
_____
_____

APPLICATION

_____
_____
_____

CHALLENGE

_____
_____
_____
_____
_____

EMBRACE IN PRAYER

DAY 4

ENGAGE IN SCRIPTURE

_____

_____

_____

_____

MAIN THEME OF PASSAGE

_____

_____

_____

_____

BREAK IT DOWN

_____

_____

_____

_____

REVELATION

_____
_____
_____
_____
_____

APPLICATION

_____
_____
_____

CHALLENGE

_____
_____
_____
_____
_____

EMBRACE IN PRAYER

DAY 5

_____

_____

_____

_____

MAIN THEME OF PASSAGE

_____

_____

_____

_____

BREAK IT DOWN

_____

_____

_____

_____

REVELATION

_____
_____
_____
_____
_____

APPLICATION

_____
_____
_____

CHALLENGE

_____
_____
_____
_____
_____

EMBRACE IN PRAYER

DAY 6

ENGAGE IN
SCRIPTURE

_____

_____

_____

_____

MAIN THEME OF
PASSAGE

_____

_____

_____

_____

BREAK IT DOWN

_____

_____

_____

_____

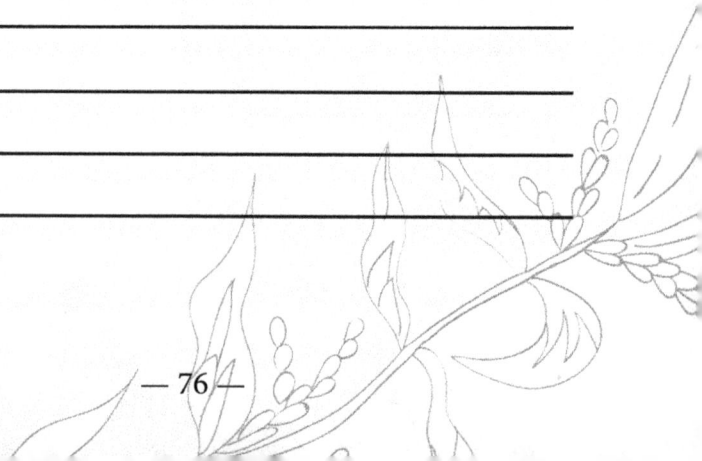

REVELATION

_____
_____
_____
_____
_____

APPLICATION

_____
_____
_____

CHALLENGE

_____
_____
_____
_____
_____

EMBRACE IN PRAYER

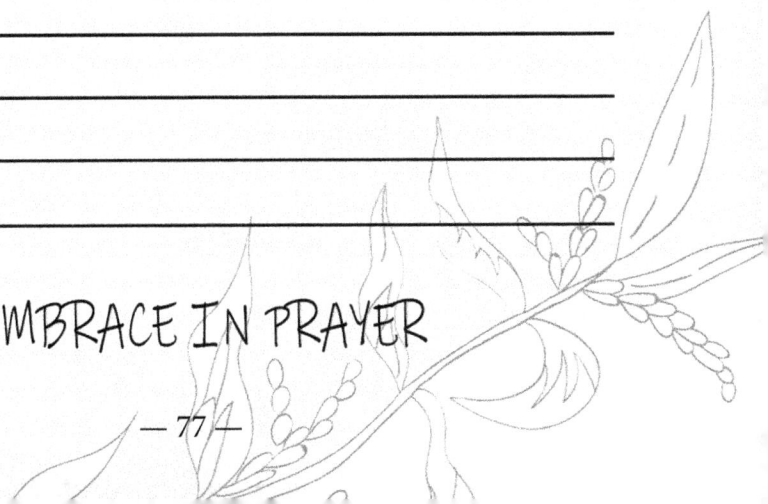

ENGAGE IN SCRIPTURE

_____
_____
_____
_____

MAIN THEME OF PASSAGE

_____
_____
_____
_____

BREAK IT DOWN

_____
_____
_____
_____

REVELATION

_____
_____
_____
_____
_____

APPLICATION

_____
_____
_____

CHALLENGE

_____
_____
_____
_____
_____

EMBRACE IN PRAYER

The Lord is my portion or share, says my living being (my inner self); therefore will I hope in Him and wait expectantly for Him. The Lord is good to those who wait hopefully and expectantly for Him, to those who seek Him [inquire of and for Him and require Him by right of necessity and on the authority of God's word].

— Lamentations 3:24-25, AMPC

Week
5

DAY 1

ENGAGE IN SCRIPTURE

_____

_____

_____

_____

MAIN THEME OF PASSAGE

_____

_____

_____

_____

BREAK IT DOWN

_____

_____

_____

_____

REVELATION

_____
_____
_____
_____
_____

APPLICATION

_____
_____
_____

CHALLENGE

_____
_____
_____
_____
_____

EMBRACE IN PRAYER

DAY 2

ENGAGE IN SCRIPTURE

_____

_____

_____

_____

MAIN THEME OF PASSAGE

_____

_____

_____

_____

BREAK IT DOWN

_____

_____

_____

_____

REVELATION

_____
_____
_____
_____
_____

APPLICATION

_____
_____
_____

CHALLENGE

_____
_____
_____
_____
_____

EMBRACE IN PRAYER

DAY 3

_____

_____

_____

_____

MAIN THEME OF PASSAGE

_____

_____

_____

_____

BREAK IT DOWN

_____

_____

_____

_____

REVELATION

_____
_____
_____
_____
_____

APPLICATION

_____
_____
_____

CHALLENGE

_____
_____
_____
_____
_____

EMBRACE IN PRAYER

ENGAGE IN SCRIPTURE

_____
_____
_____
_____

MAIN THEME OF PASSAGE

_____
_____
_____
_____

BREAK IT DOWN

_____
_____
_____
_____

REVELATION

_____
_____
_____
_____
_____

APPLICATION

_____
_____

CHALLENGE

_____
_____
_____
_____
_____

EMBRACE IN PRAYER

DAY 5

ENGAGE IN SCRIPTURE

_____
_____
_____
_____

MAIN THEME OF PASSAGE

_____
_____
_____
_____

BREAK IT DOWN

_____
_____
_____
_____

REVELATION

_____
_____
_____
_____
_____

APPLICATION

_____
_____
_____

CHALLENGE

_____
_____
_____
_____
_____

EMBRACE IN PRAYER

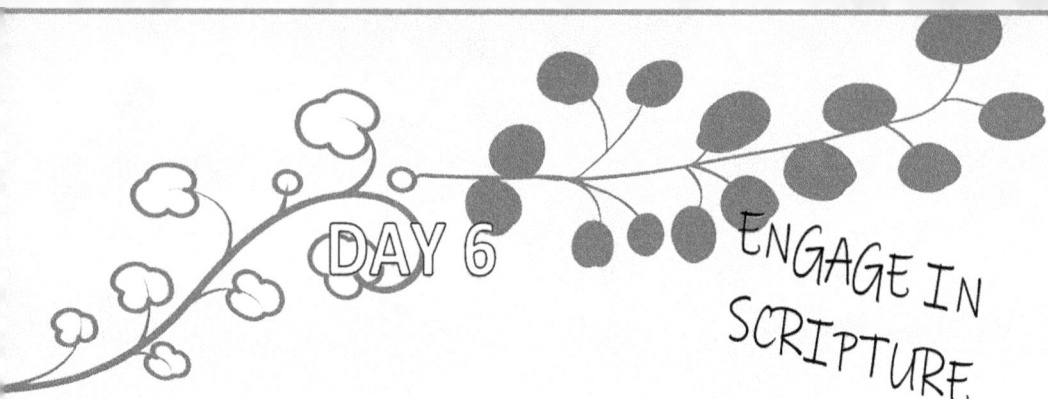

DAY 6

ENGAGE IN SCRIPTURE

_____

_____

_____

_____

MAIN THEME OF PASSAGE

_____

_____

_____

_____

BREAK IT DOWN

_____

_____

_____

_____

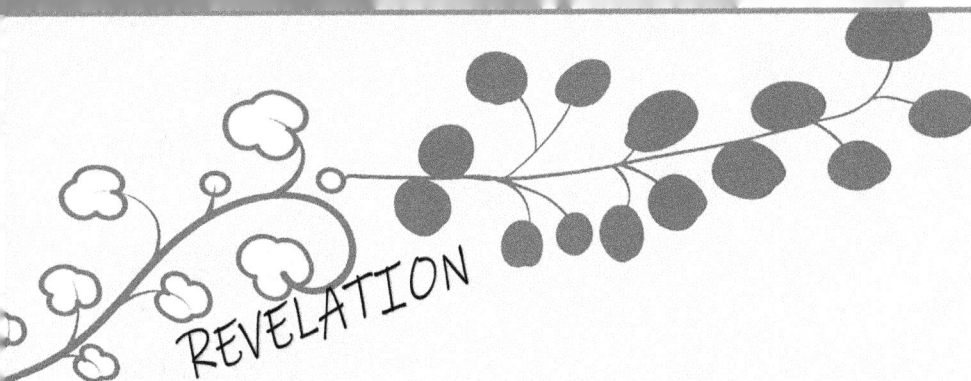

REVELATION

_____
_____
_____
_____
_____

APPLICATION

_____
_____
_____

CHALLENGE

_____
_____
_____
_____
_____

EMBRACE IN PRAYER

_____
_____
_____
_____

MAIN THEME OF PASSAGE

_____
_____
_____
_____

BREAK IT DOWN

_____
_____
_____
_____

REVELATION

_____
_____
_____
_____
_____

APPLICATION

_____
_____
_____

CHALLENGE

_____
_____
_____
_____
_____

EMBRACE IN PRAYER

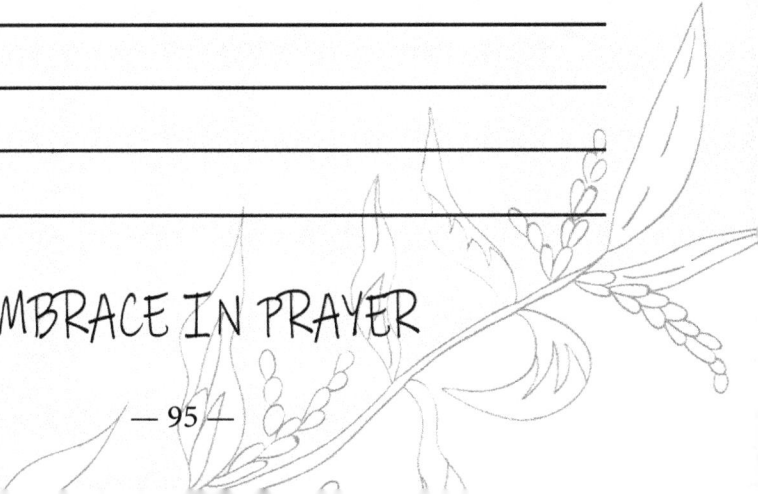

Your words were found, and I ate them; and Your words were to me a joy and the rejoicing of my heart, for I am called by Your name, O LORD God of hosts.

— Jeremiah 15:16, AMPC

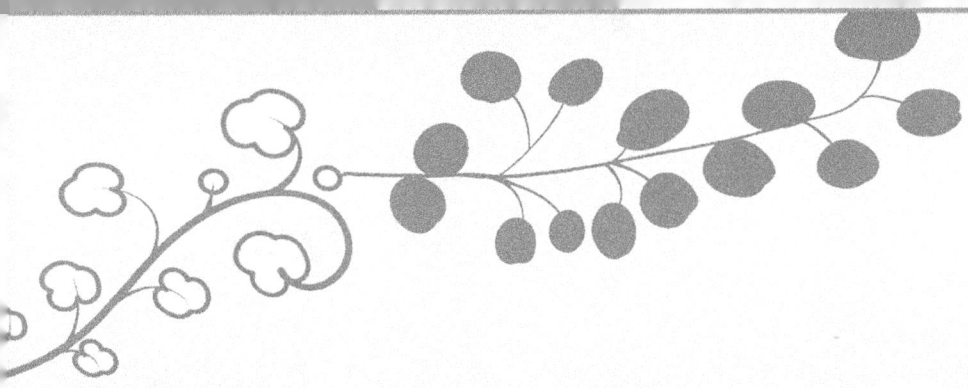

week

6

DAY 1

ENGAGE IN SCRIPTURE

_____
_____
_____
_____

MAIN THEME OF PASSAGE

_____
_____
_____
_____

BREAK IT DOWN

_____
_____
_____
_____

REVELATION

_____

_____

_____

_____

_____

APPLICATION

_____

_____

_____

CHALLENGE

_____

_____

_____

_____

_____

EMBRACE IN PRAYER

DAY 2

_____
_____
_____
_____

MAIN THEME OF PASSAGE

_____
_____
_____
_____

BREAK IT DOWN

_____
_____
_____
_____

REVELATION

_____
_____
_____
_____
_____

APPLICATION

_____
_____
_____

CHALLENGE

_____
_____
_____
_____
_____

EMBRACE IN PRAYER

DAY 3

_____

_____

_____

_____

MAIN THEME OF PASSAGE

_____

_____

_____

_____

BREAK IT DOWN

_____

_____

_____

_____

REVELATION

_____
_____
_____
_____
_____

APPLICATION

_____
_____
_____

CHALLENGE

_____
_____
_____
_____
_____

EMBRACE IN PRAYER

DAY 4
ENGAGE IN SCRIPTURE

_____
_____
_____
_____

MAIN THEME OF PASSAGE

_____
_____
_____
_____

BREAK IT DOWN

_____
_____
_____
_____

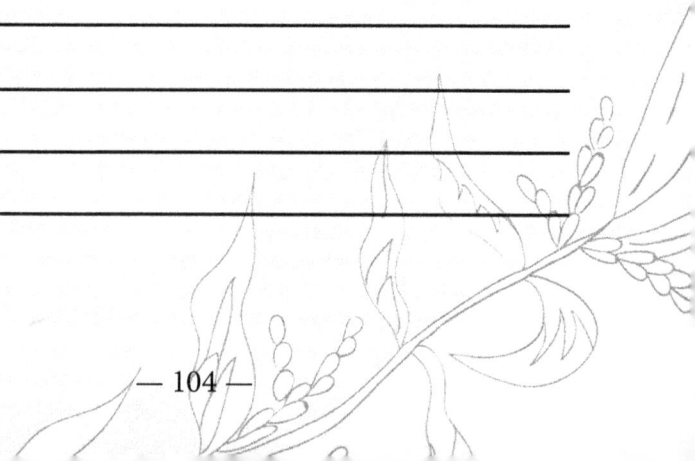

REVELATION

_____

_____

_____

_____

_____

APPLICATION

_____

_____

_____

CHALLENGE

_____

_____

_____

_____

_____

EMBRACE IN PRAYER

DAY 5

ENGAGE IN SCRIPTURE

_____
_____
_____
_____

MAIN THEME OF PASSAGE

_____
_____
_____
_____

BREAK IT DOWN

_____
_____
_____
_____

REVELATION

_____
_____
_____
_____
_____

APPLICATION

_____
_____
_____

CHALLENGE

_____
_____
_____
_____
_____

EMBRACE IN PRAYER

DAY 6

ENGAGE IN SCRIPTURE

_____
_____
_____
_____

MAIN THEME OF PASSAGE

_____
_____
_____
_____

BREAK IT DOWN

_____
_____
_____
_____

REVELATION

_____
_____
_____
_____
_____

APPLICATION

_____
_____
_____

CHALLENGE

_____
_____
_____
_____
_____

EMBRACE IN PRAYER

_____
_____
_____
_____

MAIN THEME OF PASSAGE

_____
_____
_____
_____

BREAK IT DOWN

_____
_____
_____
_____

REVELATION

_____
_____
_____
_____
_____

APPLICATION

_____
_____
_____

CHALLENGE

_____
_____
_____
_____
_____

EMBRACE IN PRAYER

Jesus answered by quoting Deuteronomy: "It takes more than bread to stay alive. It takes a steady stream of words from God's mouth."
— Matthew 4:4, MSG

week

7

DAY 1

ENGAGE IN SCRIPTURE

_____

_____

_____

_____

MAIN THEME OF PASSAGE

_____

_____

_____

_____

BREAK IT DOWN

_____

_____

_____

_____

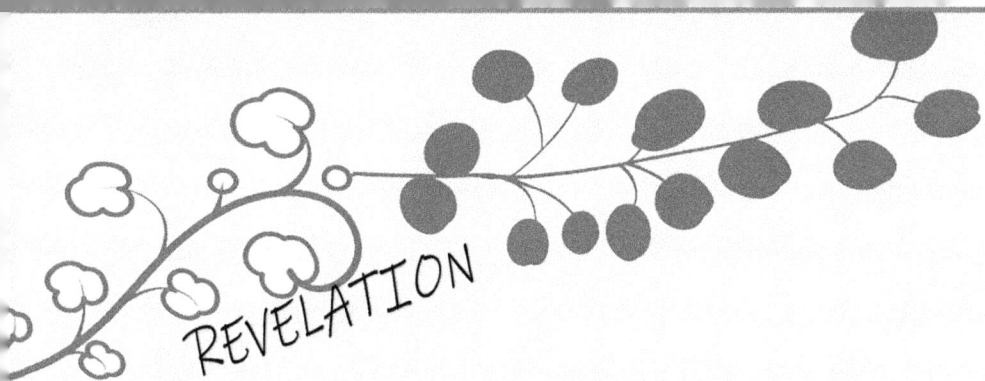

REVELATION

_____
_____
_____
_____
_____

APPLICATION

_____
_____
_____

CHALLENGE

_____
_____
_____
_____
_____

EMBRACE IN PRAYER

DAY 2

_____

_____

_____

_____

MAIN THEME OF PASSAGE

_____

_____

_____

_____

BREAK IT DOWN

_____

_____

_____

_____

REVELATION

_____
_____
_____
_____
_____

APPLICATION

_____
_____

CHALLENGE

_____
_____
_____
_____
_____

EMBRACE IN PRAYER

DAY 3

_____
_____
_____
_____

MAIN THEME OF PASSAGE

_____
_____
_____
_____

BREAK IT DOWN

_____
_____
_____
_____

REVELATION

_____

_____

_____

_____

_____

APPLICATION

_____

_____

_____

CHALLENGE

_____

_____

_____

_____

_____

EMBRACE IN PRAYER

ENGAGE IN SCRIPTURE

_____
_____
_____
_____

MAIN THEME OF PASSAGE

_____
_____
_____
_____

BREAK IT DOWN

_____
_____
_____
_____

REVELATION

_____
_____
_____
_____
_____

APPLICATION

_____
_____
_____

CHALLENGE

_____
_____
_____
_____
_____

EMBRACE IN PRAYER

DAY 5

ENGAGE IN
SCRIPTURE

_____
_____
_____
_____

MAIN THEME OF
PASSAGE

_____
_____
_____
_____

BREAK IT DOWN

_____
_____
_____
_____

REVELATION

_____
_____
_____
_____
_____

APPLICATION

_____
_____
_____

CHALLENGE

_____
_____
_____
_____
_____

EMBRACE IN PRAYER

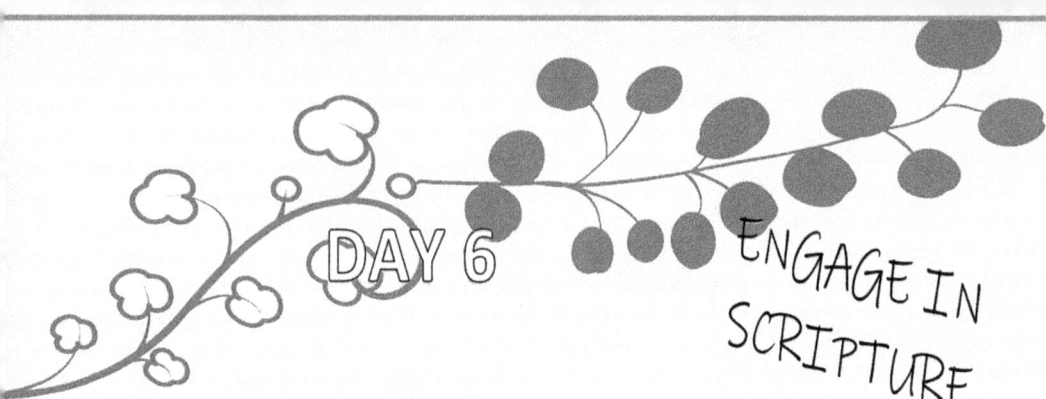

DAY 6

ENGAGE IN SCRIPTURE

_____
_____
_____
_____

MAIN THEME OF PASSAGE

_____
_____
_____
_____

BREAK IT DOWN

_____
_____
_____
_____

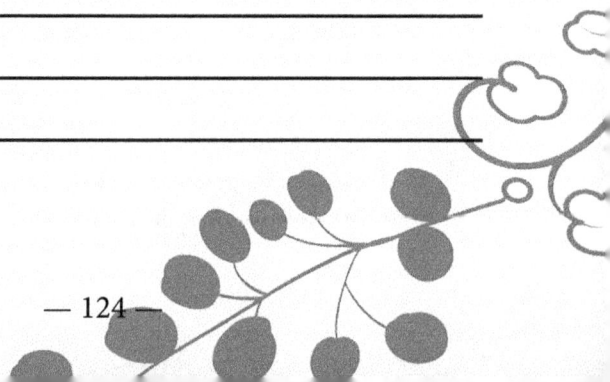

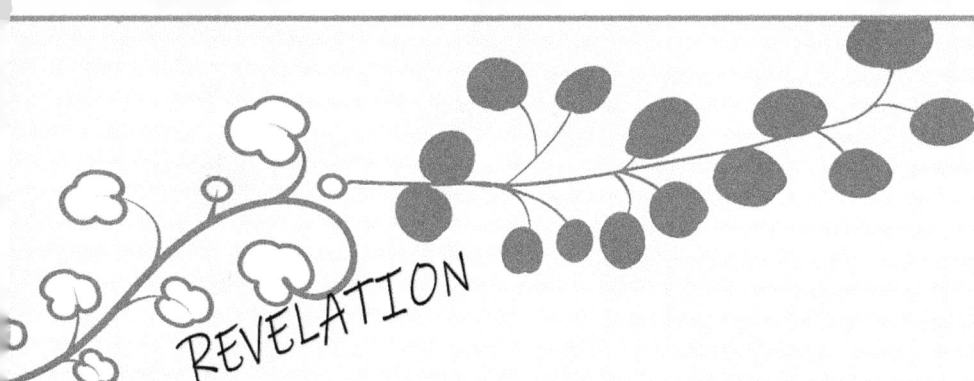

REVELATION

_____
_____
_____
_____
_____

APPLICATION

_____
_____
_____

CHALLENGE

_____
_____
_____
_____
_____

EMBRACE IN PRAYER

ENGAGE IN
SCRIPTURE

_____
_____
_____
_____

MAIN THEME OF
PASSAGE

_____
_____
_____
_____

BREAK IT DOWN

_____
_____
_____
_____

REVELATION

_____
_____
_____
_____
_____

APPLICATION

_____
_____
_____

CHALLENGE

_____
_____
_____
_____
_____

EMBRACE IN PRAYER

Thus says the LORD, the God of Israel: Write all the words that I have spoken to you in a book.
— Jeremiah 30:2, AMPC

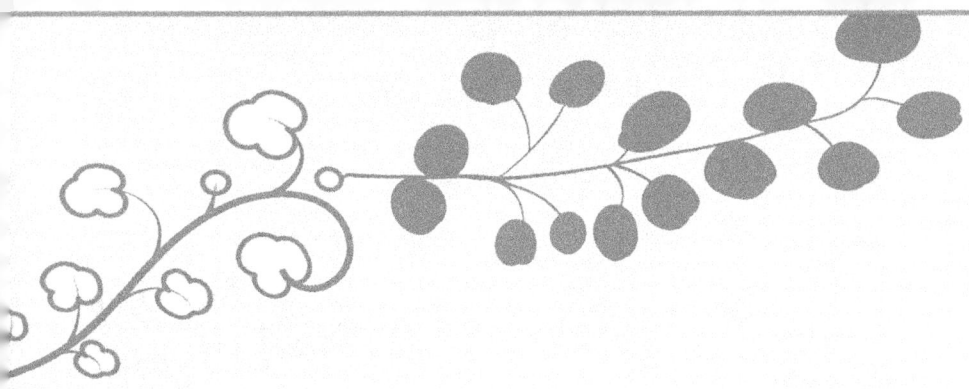

Week

8

DAY 1

ENGAGE IN SCRIPTURE

_____

_____

_____

_____

MAIN THEME OF PASSAGE

_____

_____

_____

_____

BREAK IT DOWN

_____

_____

_____

_____

REVELATION

_____

_____

_____

_____

_____

APPLICATION

_____

_____

_____

CHALLENGE

_____

_____

_____

_____

_____

EMBRACE IN PRAYER

DAY 2

ENGAGE IN SCRIPTURE

_____
_____
_____
_____

MAIN THEME OF PASSAGE

_____
_____
_____
_____

BREAK IT DOWN

_____
_____
_____
_____

REVELATION

_____
_____
_____
_____
_____

APPLICATION

_____
_____
_____

CHALLENGE

_____
_____
_____
_____
_____

EMBRACE IN PRAYER

DAY 3

ENGAGE IN SCRIPTURE

_____

_____

_____

_____

MAIN THEME OF PASSAGE

_____

_____

_____

_____

BREAK IT DOWN

_____

_____

_____

_____

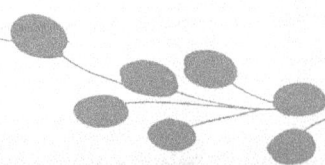

REVELATION

_____
_____
_____
_____
_____

APPLICATION

_____
_____
_____

CHALLENGE

_____
_____
_____
_____
_____

EMBRACE IN PRAYER

DAY 4

ENGAGE IN SCRIPTURE

_____
_____
_____
_____

MAIN THEME OF PASSAGE

_____
_____
_____
_____

BREAK IT DOWN

_____
_____
_____
_____

REVELATION

_____
_____
_____
_____
_____

APPLICATION

_____
_____
_____

CHALLENGE

_____
_____
_____
_____
_____

EMBRACE IN PRAYER

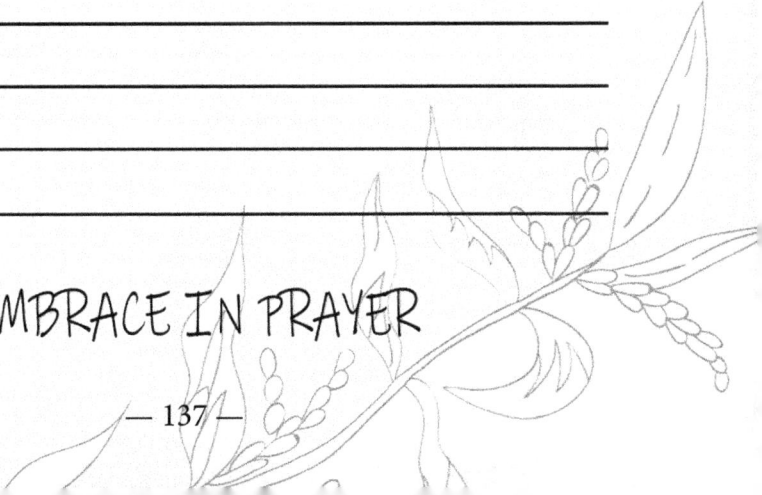

DAY 5

ENGAGE IN SCRIPTURE

_____
_____
_____
_____

MAIN THEME OF PASSAGE

_____
_____
_____
_____

BREAK IT DOWN

_____
_____
_____
_____

REVELATION

_____
_____
_____
_____
_____

APPLICATION

_____
_____
_____

CHALLENGE

_____
_____
_____
_____
_____

EMBRACE IN PRAYER

DAY 6

ENGAGE IN SCRIPTURE

_____
_____
_____
_____

MAIN THEME OF PASSAGE

_____
_____
_____
_____

BREAK IT DOWN

_____
_____
_____
_____

REVELATION

_____
_____
_____
_____
_____

APPLICATION

_____
_____
_____

CHALLENGE

_____
_____
_____
_____
_____

EMBRACE IN PRAYER

ENGAGE IN SCRIPTURE

_____
_____
_____
_____

MAIN THEME OF PASSAGE

_____
_____
_____
_____

BREAK IT DOWN

_____
_____
_____
_____

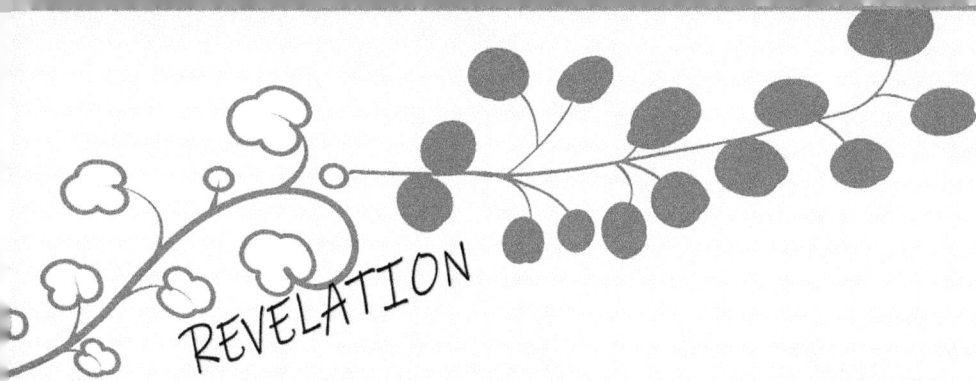

REVELATION

_____

_____

_____

_____

_____

APPLICATION

_____

_____

_____

CHALLENGE

_____

_____

_____

_____

_____

EMBRACE IN PRAYER

So don't hide your light! Let it shine brightly before others, so that the commendable things you do will shine as light upon them, and they will give their praise to your Father in heaven.

— Matthew 5:16, TPT

week

9

DAY 1

ENGAGE IN SCRIPTURE

_____
_____
_____
_____

MAIN THEME OF PASSAGE

_____
_____
_____
_____

BREAK IT DOWN

_____
_____
_____
_____

REVELATION

_____
_____
_____
_____
_____

APPLICATION

_____
_____
_____

CHALLENGE

_____
_____
_____
_____
_____

EMBRACE IN PRAYER

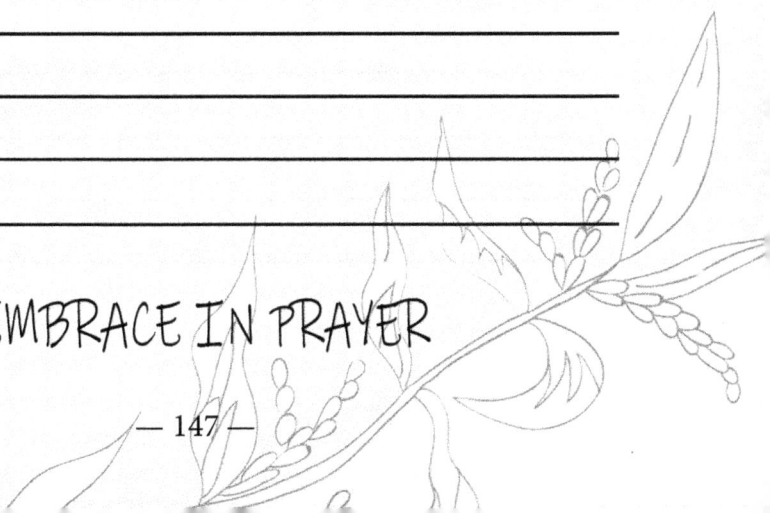

DAY 2

_____
_____
_____
_____

MAIN THEME OF PASSAGE

_____
_____
_____
_____

BREAK IT DOWN

_____
_____
_____
_____

REVELATION

_____
_____
_____
_____
_____

APPLICATION

_____
_____
_____

CHALLENGE

_____
_____
_____
_____
_____

EMBRACE IN PRAYER

DAY 3

ENGAGE IN
SCRIPTURE

_____
_____
_____
_____

MAIN THEME OF PASSAGE

_____
_____
_____
_____

BREAK IT DOWN

_____
_____
_____
_____

REVELATION

_____
_____
_____
_____
_____

APPLICATION

_____
_____
_____

CHALLENGE

_____
_____
_____
_____
_____

EMBRACE IN PRAYER

DAY 4

ENGAGE IN SCRIPTURE

_____
_____
_____
_____

MAIN THEME OF PASSAGE

_____
_____
_____
_____

BREAK IT DOWN

_____
_____
_____
_____

REVELATION

_____

_____

_____

_____

_____

APPLICATION

_____

_____

_____

CHALLENGE

_____

_____

_____

_____

_____

EMBRACE IN PRAYER

DAY 5

ENGAGE IN
SCRIPTURE

_____
_____
_____
_____

MAIN THEME OF
PASSAGE

_____
_____
_____
_____

BREAK IT DOWN

_____
_____
_____
_____

REVELATION

_____
_____
_____
_____
_____

APPLICATION

_____
_____
_____

CHALLENGE

_____
_____
_____
_____
_____

EMBRACE IN PRAYER

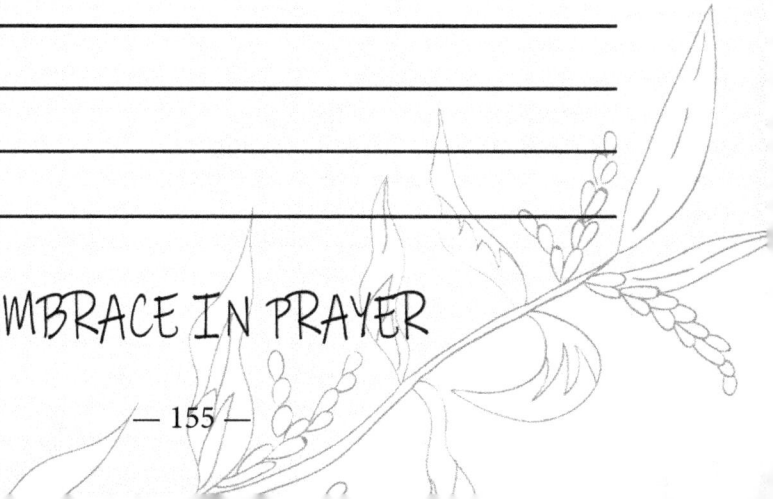

DAY 6

ENGAGE IN SCRIPTURE

_____
_____
_____
_____

MAIN THEME OF PASSAGE

_____
_____
_____
_____

BREAK IT DOWN

_____
_____
_____
_____

REVELATION

_____
_____
_____
_____
_____

APPLICATION

_____
_____
_____

CHALLENGE

_____
_____
_____
_____
_____

EMBRACE IN PRAYER

ENGAGE IN
SCRIPTURE

_____
_____
_____
_____

MAIN THEME OF
PASSAGE

_____
_____
_____
_____

BREAK IT DOWN

_____
_____
_____
_____

REVELATION

_____
_____
_____
_____
_____

APPLICATION

_____
_____
_____

CHALLENGE

_____
_____
_____
_____
_____

EMBRACE IN PRAYER

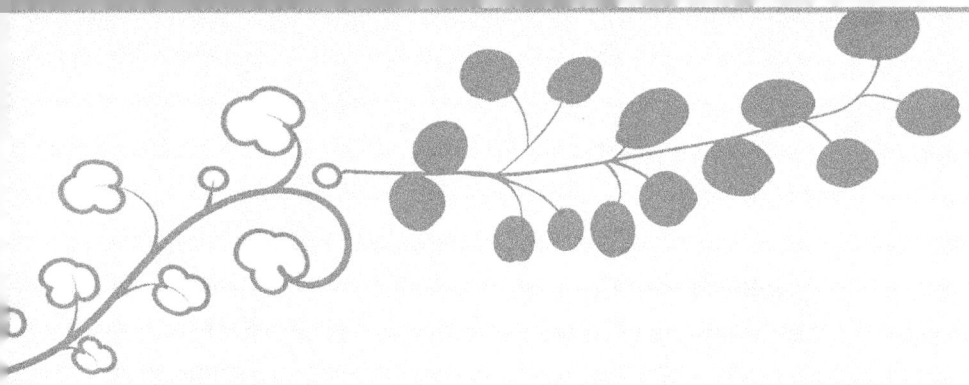

Sermon Notes

SERMON NOTES

Date: /   /

_____
_____
_____
_____
_____
_____
_____
_____
_____
_____
_____
_____
_____
_____
_____
_____
_____
_____
_____
_____
_____
_____
_____
_____
_____

What I learned from the sermon? _____
_____
_____

Key verses or thoughts to further study on?_____
_____
_____

SERMON NOTES

Date: / /

_____
_____
_____
_____
_____
_____
_____
_____
_____
_____
_____
_____
_____
_____
_____
_____
_____
_____
_____
_____
_____
_____
_____
_____
_____

What I learned from the sermon? _____
_____
_____

Key verses or thoughts to further study on?_____
_____
_____

SERMON NOTES

Date: / /

_____
_____
_____
_____
_____
_____
_____
_____
_____
_____
_____
_____
_____
_____
_____
_____
_____
_____
_____
_____
_____
_____
_____
_____
_____

What I learned from the sermon? _____
_____
_____

Key verses or thoughts to further study on?_____
_____
_____

SERMON NOTES

Date: / /

_____
_____
_____
_____
_____
_____
_____
_____
_____
_____
_____
_____
_____
_____
_____
_____
_____
_____
_____
_____
_____
_____
_____
_____
_____
_____

What I learned from the sermon? _____
_____
_____

Key verses or thoughts to further study on?_____
_____
_____

SERMON NOTES

Date: /   /

_____
_____
_____
_____
_____
_____
_____
_____
_____
_____
_____
_____
_____
_____
_____
_____
_____
_____
_____
_____
_____
_____
_____
_____
_____
_____

What I learned from the sermon? _____
_____
_____

Key verses or thoughts to further study on?_____
_____
_____

SERMON NOTES

Date: /   /

_____
_____
_____
_____
_____
_____
_____
_____
_____
_____
_____
_____
_____
_____
_____
_____
_____
_____
_____
_____
_____
_____
_____
_____
_____
_____
_____
_____

What I learned from the sermon? _____
_____
_____

Key verses or thoughts to further study on?_____
_____
_____

SERMON NOTES

Date: /   /

_____
_____
_____
_____
_____
_____
_____
_____
_____
_____
_____
_____
_____
_____
_____
_____
_____
_____
_____
_____
_____
_____
_____
_____

What I learned from the sermon? _____
_____
_____

Key verses or thoughts to further study on?_____
_____
_____

SERMON NOTES

Date: / /

_____
_____
_____
_____
_____
_____
_____
_____
_____
_____
_____
_____
_____
_____
_____
_____
_____
_____
_____
_____
_____
_____
_____
_____
_____
_____
_____
_____

What I learned from the sermon? _____
_____
_____

Key verses or thoughts to further study on?_____
_____
_____

SERMON NOTES

Date: /   /

_____
_____
_____
_____
_____
_____
_____
_____
_____
_____
_____
_____
_____
_____
_____
_____
_____
_____
_____
_____
_____
_____
_____
_____
_____
_____

What I learned from the sermon? _____
_____
_____

Key verses or thoughts to further study on?_____
_____
_____

SERMON NOTES

Date: /   /

_____
_____
_____
_____
_____
_____
_____
_____
_____
_____
_____
_____
_____
_____
_____
_____
_____
_____
_____
_____
_____
_____
_____
_____

What I learned from the sermon? _____
_____
_____

Key verses or thoughts to further study on?_____
_____
_____

SERMON NOTES

Date: /   /

_____
_____
_____
_____
_____
_____
_____
_____
_____
_____
_____
_____
_____
_____
_____
_____
_____
_____
_____
_____
_____
_____
_____
_____
_____
_____

What I learned from the sermon? _____
_____
_____

Key verses or thoughts to further study on?_____
_____
_____

SERMON NOTES

Date:　　/　　/

_____
_____
_____
_____
_____
_____
_____
_____
_____
_____
_____
_____
_____
_____
_____
_____
_____
_____
_____
_____
_____
_____
_____
_____
_____
_____

What I learned from the sermon? _____

_____

_____

Key verses or thoughts to further study on?_____

_____

_____

SERMON NOTES

Date: / /

_____
_____
_____
_____
_____
_____
_____
_____
_____
_____
_____
_____
_____
_____
_____
_____
_____
_____
_____
_____
_____
_____
_____
_____
_____
_____

What I learned from the sermon? _____
_____
_____

Key verses or thoughts to further study on?_____
_____
_____

SERMON NOTES

Date: /   /

_____
_____
_____
_____
_____
_____
_____
_____
_____
_____
_____
_____
_____
_____
_____
_____
_____
_____
_____
_____
_____
_____
_____
_____
_____

What I learned from the sermon? _____
_____
_____

Key verses or thoughts to further study on?_____
_____
_____

SERMON NOTES

Date: /   /

_____
_____
_____
_____
_____
_____
_____
_____
_____
_____
_____
_____
_____
_____
_____
_____
_____
_____
_____
_____
_____
_____
_____
_____
_____
_____
_____
_____

What I learned from the sermon? _____
_____
_____

Key verses or thoughts to further study on?_____
_____
_____

SERMON NOTES

Date: /   /

_____
_____
_____
_____
_____
_____
_____
_____
_____
_____
_____
_____
_____
_____
_____
_____
_____
_____
_____
_____
_____
_____
_____
_____

What I learned from the sermon? _____

_____

_____

Key verses or thoughts to further study on?_____

_____

_____

SERMON NOTES

Date: / /

_____
_____
_____
_____
_____
_____
_____
_____
_____
_____
_____
_____
_____
_____
_____
_____
_____
_____
_____
_____
_____
_____
_____
_____
_____

What I learned from the sermon? _____
_____
_____

Key verses or thoughts to further study on?_____
_____
_____

SERMON NOTES

Date: /   /

_____
_____
_____
_____
_____
_____
_____
_____
_____
_____
_____
_____
_____
_____
_____
_____
_____
_____
_____
_____
_____
_____
_____
_____
_____
_____

What I learned from the sermon? _____
_____
_____

Key verses or thoughts to further study on?_____
_____
_____

ABOUT THE AUTHOR

Crystal Callais has been happily married to Russell Callais for more than twenty years and is the mother of three beautiful daughters whom she homeschools. Since 2016, she has been heavily involved in various ministries in her home church that she has been a part of for more than twenty-five years. She has authored several other books, one of which is a freedom curriculum that is being used in her home church. She is currently the Next Gen Pastor, overseeing children's ministry from birth until 19 years of age. Her desire is that, as you spend time with the Father in His Word daily, you would feel the embrace of the Father in the deepest parts of your being. She says, "There is so much that happens in our lives and the lives of those we come in contact with when we spend time in the presence of the Father and allow Him to speak and direct us."

OTHER BOOKS BY CRYSTAL CALLAIS

Do you find yourself struggling with unanswered prayers and unanswered questions? With family unity? With fulfilling your call in God? With maintaining your peace, assurance, self-worth, or self-respect? Are you looking for a deeper, more intimate walk with Jesus Christ, your Lord and Savior? Join us as we journey from Genesis through Revelation, allowing the Holy Spirit to reveal to us a deeper understanding of who the Lord truly is; He is LOVE!

We will discuss patterns, mindsets and broken covenants that stand in our way, preventing us from fully experiencing what is ours. Our hope is that you will see how these mindsets, which are strongholds, pass from one generation to the next and how to stop them in their tracks and not allow them to continue down your family line.

Total freedom is possible for you! Through this course, you will learn how to maintain the freedom that was purchased at such a high price with the BLOOD of Jesus Christ on the cross of Calvary.

Maintaining Generational FREEDOM

— STUDENT MANUAL —

Crystal Callais
and
Lorraine Foret

There are times in our lives when we become stagnant and have a hard time breaking the repetitiveness that we have fallen into. This devotional was inspired to aid in bringing a fresh and deeper thought process into the study of God's Word. His will is that we continually have a fresh revelation of Him and see everything from His perspective, not our own. Crystal has included questions that will challenge you to think outside of your normal thought process or "out of the box." Allow every part of this devotional to be thought provoking, while positioning yourself to be vulnerable before God. If you do that, He will bring you into new depths in your relationship with Him, and you will find yourself *Going Deeper.*

Going Deeper

A 90-Day Devotional

Crystal Callais

We all have a boat of comfort we tend to navigate life through, and there are moments in life when the Lord God calls us to step out of our comfort zone and do things we are not always comfortable with. At times, the water is calm and peaceful, so stepping out of the boat in obedience to what He has asked of us is easy. But what if there is a storm present? What if the water seems rough, making it harder to step out of our comfort zone when the Lord asks us to? In these times, we need to grow and stretch our faith in the Lord God so that we can step out in obedience. Take this journey and grow your faith. This study can be used with some friends as a small group study or as a personal growth plan. Crystal will lead you through scripture references and stories to help build your faith, enabling you to step out the boat of your comfort when the Lord God calls you out.

Stepping Out of the BOAT

A Study on Faith

Crystal Callais

Foreword by Joshua Mills

Author Contact Page

You may contact Crystal Callais directly at:

maintainingfreedom@yahoo.com